D1157427

1. *Kempenfelt*, *Mounsey* and *Rob Roy*, about 1917.

WARSHIPS ILLUSTRATED No 7

BRITISH DESTROYERS
in World War One

R. A. BURT

ARMS AND ARMOUR PRESS

825.5
G7
B86
1986

Published in 1986 by Arms & Armour Press Ltd.,
2–6 Hampstead High Street, London NW3 1QQ.

Distributed in the United States by Sterling
Publishing Co. Inc., 2 Park Avenue, New York,
N.Y. 10016.

British Library Cataloguing in Publication Data:
Burt, Ray
British destroyers in World War One.–
(Warships illustrated; 7)
1. Great Britain. *Royal Navy* – History
2. Destroyers (Warships) – Great Britain
– History   3. World War, 1914–1918 –
Naval operations, British
I. Title   II. Series
623.8′254′0941   V825.5.G7

ISBN 0-85368-753-6

Editing, design and artwork by Roger Chesneau.
Typesetting by Typesetters (Birmingham) Ltd.
Printed and bound in Italy by GEA/GEP in
association with Keats European Ltd., London.

Introduction

The concept of the destroyer arose from the urgent need for an entirely new form of vessel which could rid the seas of all enemy torpedo craft, which by the late nineteenth century had reached large proportions (in terms of both size and numbers), especially in the French and Russian Navies. In an effort to counter this threat, an experimental vessel, *Rattlesnake*, was ordered by the Admiralty: launched in 1886 and officially classed as a 'torpedo boat catcher', she displaced over 500 tons and mounted one 4in gun, six machine guns and four torpedo tubes. She was thus hardly a small vessel, but her designed speed, 18kts, was insufficient to catch the French craft, which were reported to be reaching at least 23. Further construction along these lines continued until 1892, but despite many improvements the type was not successful, owing mainly to its high unit cost and its inability to overhaul a torpedo boat except in very rough weather.

The origin of the true destroyer is generally attributed to Sir Alfred Yarrow, who in the spring of 1892 approached Rear-Admiral Fisher with details of a new programme of French torpedo boats and, in addition, with proposals of his own for a vessel that could really tackle the problem. The basic design represented an enlarged version of the existing torpedo boat type, but had a heavier armament, a higher speed and better sea-keeping qualities. Originally known as a 'torpedo boat destroyer' – the word 'destroyer' is thought to have come from either William White (Director of Naval Construction) or from Fisher, who referred to 'destroying' the French and Russian boats – the prototype *Havock* was built in 1893, and from it evolved the immensely successful vessels which served the Royal Navy with exceptional valour and distinction throughout the First World War. That conflict proved the value of the concept, and ensured that these little ships would be here to stay for a very long time to come.

R. A. Burt

◄2
2. *Mentor* in trouble, following a collision. See also photograph 76.

▲3

3. The first order from the Admiralty for a torpedo-boat destroyer was given to the private yard of Messrs Yarrow of Poplar in 1893, and in October that year *Havock*, the first of her type, was launched. On completion she ran a lengthy series of trials, which proved so successful that further orders were placed with the private yards of Thornycroft and Lairds to construct two vessels each, with Yarrow being asked to prepare a sister for *Havock*. The vessels differed slightly from each other, particularly in respect of their boilers and engines, but, armed with one 12pdr (on the bridge platform), three 6pdrs (two port and starboard at the break of the turtle-back, and one on the centreline aft) and three 18in torpedo tubes, they were formidable boats. Here *Havock* is seen in about 1896. The photograph shows well her general layout: note in particular the strong, sloping stern, the stern torpedo tubes and the turtle-deck forward.

4. *Havock* in 1904, after being re-boilered and having her funnel altered.

5. Although *Hornet* was built as a sister to *Havock* she differed in appearance a great deal. This photograph, taken in 1902, shows her four funnels (the midships pair close together) and her mast stepped before the first funnel. The seaworthiness and manoeuvrability of these early torpedo boat destroyers varied to some extent,

Thornycroft boats tending, in general, to be the better seaboats. During the 1894 Manoeuvres *Havock* and *Hornet* were ordered to 'stand by' for twenty-four hours in the Bay of Biscay, and both were reported to have behaved very satisfactorily.

6. The third boat in this group was *Daring*, built by Thornycroft of Chiswick and completed in February 1895. She was fitted with water tube boilers, unlike *Havock*, which had the locomotive type. *Havock* set up a world record on her steam trials by logging 27.177kts, and for a period was the fastest warship afloat. This record, however, was short-lived, for *Hornet* (water tube boilers) made 27.6kts. Both these figures were passed when *Daring* ran her trials and reached 29.678kts. These exceptionally high speeds give a false impression of the vessels' true capabilities at sea, because the preliminary trials were run in light condition, without armament, ammunition, stores or on occasion masts; moreover, the stokers were hand-picked, and the hulls were black-leaded and polished to minimize water resistance. The photograph shows *Daring* in about 1898.

7. *Decoy* was almost identical to *Daring* but had taller funnels with steam pipes which did not extend to the rims. She was lost after colliding with *Arun* off Sicily on 13 August 1904. This photograph was taken during 1902.

▼4

5▲

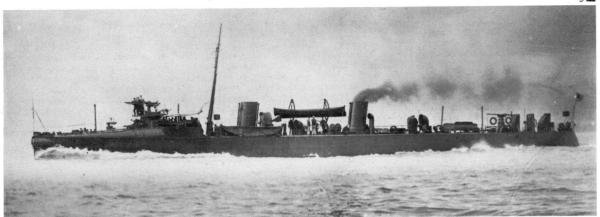

6▲   7▼

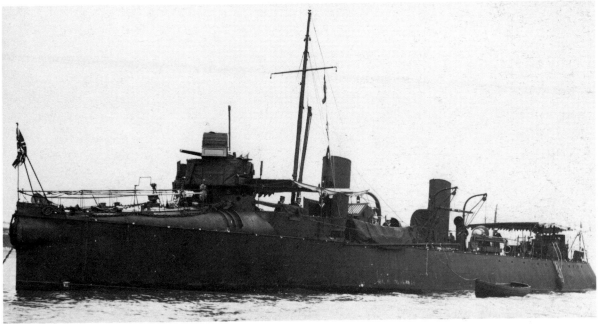

▲8 ▼9

10▲

8. *Ferret*, showing her four widely spaced funnels and sharply cut-away stern. The fixed bow torpedo tube fitted in the first six vessels was abandoned in later designs owing to the risk of a boat overtaking its own torpedo; the tube also made for considerable inconvenience in the living spaces forward. In 1909 the ship was converted for 'boom-breaking': her forward gun, forebridge and tube were removed and her forecastle was strengthened.

9. *Boxer* as completed, about 1895. Fourteen further boats were ordered in July 1893 under the 1983/94 Programme and another six a little later. The final group of sixteen were provided under the 1894/95 Programme, making a total of 42 boats, all of which were referred to as the '27-knotters'. Only the finest steel was used to construct these boats, with the hull usually ¼in to ⅜in thick, and on a bright day the framework could be clearly traced.

10, 11. After the first six torpedo boat destroyers had been completed, the armament was increased to one 12pdr and five 6pdrs, with a reduction to two 18in torpedo tubes. Special trials carried out with *Havock* during the 1894 Manoeuvres indicated that the 12pdr gun was inadequate for dealing with contemporary torpedo boats; later tests throughout the rest of the group showed that good shooting could be maintained in smooth water but fell off considerably in a seaway, although it was still classed as effective. These two photographs show *Banshee* whilst serving in the Mediterranean, 1900–02.

11▼

▲12

12. *Charger* in 1902, after she had been re-boilered. The paint schemes of these boats varied somewhat at first, and one or two of the early vessels are reported to have been greenish-brown as completed, but the majority were given black hulls and some featured a white turtle-back. Funnels and cowls were either black or yellow. An all-black scheme became standard around 1901–02, except for those vessels serving on the Mediterranean or China Stations.

13. *Hart* (shown here in 1911), *Hardy* and *Janus* served on the China Station during the whole or greater part of their careers. Note the rig fore and aft, and also the China Station colouring of white hull and buff upperworks.

14. *Dasher* was completed with locomotive type boilers and two small funnels, and reached a speed of 26.21kts with 3,182 shaft horse power; she was, however, re-boilered in 1899–1901 with water tube boilers, and, fitted with three funnels, reached 27kts on 3,888shp. The photograph shows the 12pdr on bridge, 6pdr guns at the break of the turtle-deck, the thick second funnel and the 6pdr aft.

13▲   14▼

▲15　▼16

17▲

15. *Snapper* and *Salmon*, both built by Earle, were practically identical in appearance, with four thick funnels and the mast between the first and second funnels. *Snapper* is seen here in 1902.
16. Accommodation in the '27-knotters' varied, and although some boats were better than others in this respect, generally there was a lot to be desired. *Opossum* of this group was reported to have been by far the most comfortable and roomy of them all, whereas *Daring*, *Decoy*, *Ferret* and *Lynx* were stated to be very uncomfortable, with the first two especially cramped. This is *Zebra*, 1902.

17. *Fervent*, shown here during her trials, and *Zephyr* were built as '27-knotters' by Hanna Gordon and completed in 1895. They were fitted with a single, thick funnel, produced by trunking the two uptakes together, which gave these boats a much more pleasing appearance than the rest of the group. However, the two vessels did not enter service for some time after their completion owing to the fact that they never reached their contract speed with their original locomotive boilers. They were finally accepted in 1900–01 after receiving water tube boilers and being fitted with four thin funnels.

▲18 ▼19

18. The first '30-knotters' were laid down under the 1894/95 Supplementary Programme and the last under the 1900/01 Programme. There were seventy of these boats in all, designed by individual builders to basic Admiralty requirements. In practice they were little more than enlarged and faster '27-knotters', the main trend in the design being towards higher speed but showing no increase in offensive power. Owing to their age, only eleven of the '27-knotters' entered the war in 1914, but 65 of the '30-knotters' saw service during the conflict, ten being lost by 1918.

19. As a result of sea experience with the '27-knotters', the '30-knotters' were generally more strongly constructed, but they nevertheless still proved somewhat weak for the service that was required from them. *Orwell* was completed by Lairds in 1900 and is seen here after her collision with HMS *Pioneer* in the Ionian Sea on 5 January 1903 when she sustained 15 casualties. She served with the Grand Fleet (7th Flotilla) from 1914 until 1917, and then on patrol duties in the Irish Sea until the end of the war. She was finally sold in 1920.

20. Built by Vickers and completed in March 1900, *Otter* is seen here in 1910 on the China Station, where she served from 1900 to 1914. The boat suffered a serious boiler explosion in August 1909 at Wei-Hai and was never fully effective again, even after extensive refit. She was finally put on the disposal list in Hong Kong in March 1915.

20 ▼

▲21   ▼22

21. An excellent photograph of *Bat*, taken in about 1910. The '27-knotters' were redesignated the 'A' class in October 1913, and the '30-knotters' became the 'B', 'C' and 'D' classes (although they were always referred to as '30-knotters' in service). The 1913 groupings were arranged according to the number of funnels in each boat, the 'B' class having four, the 'C' class three and the 'Ds' two. In service the '30-knotters' could only reach their maximum speed under favourable conditions, and very few could maintain 30kts for any length of time. *Bat* was identical in appearance to *Chamois, Crane, Fawn, Flirt, Flying Fish, Star* and *Whiting*.

22. *Seal*, seen shortly before the outbreak of war, at the Fleet Review held at Spithead on 10 July 1914. Note the four very short, evenly but widely spaced funnels, and the 20in searchlight on the bridge (mounted here from 1905).

23. *Star* on 10 July 1914. The increase to 30kts in this class had been influenced by the performance of the French *Forban* (31kts) and the Russian *Sokel* (30.28kts), built by Yarrow.

24. *Stag*, photographed during her first year in the Mediterranean (where she served from 1902 to 1913) in 1902–03. Built by Thornycroft, she was one of the better-looking ships of the class.

25. *Arab, Albatross* and *Express* were experimental boats, designed to attain 32–33kts with reciprocating engines. Unfortunately, owing partly to the weight of extra hull stiffeners added whilst under construction, they never reached the high figure expected of them: *Express*, the heaviest of the group at 550 tons in the normal load condition, made 31.021kts on trials (when this photo was taken).

▲ 26

▲ 27

26. Following the remarkable speed shown by Sir Charles Parsons' *Turbinia* in 1897, the Admiralty placed an order in 1899 with the Parsons Marine Turbine Company for a turbine-driven destroyer and in May 1900 purchased a similar vessel which had been laid down by Armstrong-Whitworth in 1898 as a speculative ship for the same concern. The first of these boats was named *Viper* and the second *Cobra*; the latter is shown here running preliminary trials, when she attained speeds of up to 35.6kts on 12,000shp.

▼ 28

27, 28. *Viper* and *Cobra* were purely experimental and intended generally to provide data for future steam turbine installations, although apart from their novel machinery they were practically identical to the contemporary reciprocating-engined '30-knotters'. The trials showed that both ships were more than satisfactory, and each exceeded their nominal speeds, making them the fastest warships in the world. The photographs show *Viper* on trials.

29▲

30▲

29. Both *Viper* and *Cobra* met with unfortunate ends. *Cobra* broke in two on 18 September 1901 during heavy weather en route from the Tyne to Portsmouth to complete for service; *Viper*, seen here during 1901, was wrecked on Renouquent Island near Alderney during exercises in the fog on 3 August 1901.

30. *Blackwater* was one of the 34 *River* class boats provided under the 1901/05 Estimates. Sea experience with the '30-knotters', together with the loss of *Cobra*, had indicated that these boats were too lightly constructed to stand up to the duties demanded of them – duties which were more arduous than had been contemplated when the destroyer type was first introduced. A committee on destroyer

designs was set up by the Admiralty in November 1901 to consider future construction and the *Rivers* were a direct result of its conclusions. *Blackwater* is shown here in 1903, during her trials.

31. It was anticipated that the *Rivers* would reach 27–27½kts on 7,500shp, but a strong body of opinion considered that this speed was generally too low for destroyer work because the boats would be unable to overhaul many of the contemporary foreign torpedo boats, except in smooth water. In service, however, these destroyers proved that they could easily out-steam the earlier boats in a seaway, thanks to their high forecastle. This is *Welland*, in 1910 or 1911.

31▼

▲32

▲33 ▼34

35▲

32. *Chelmer* was one of the *River*s built by Thornycroft and was completed in 1905. She had her bottom blown out by shellfire on 18 March 1915 during the Dardanelles campaign whilst taking on survivors from the sunken battleship *Irresistible*. She was repaired at Malta and survived the war to be sold in June 1920.

33. In October 1913 the *River*s were redesignated the 'E' class, but in service they were always referred to as 'the Rivers'. *Exe*, in about 1908–09, shows that the forward 6pdrs are in sponsons, a feature of the first eighteen boats designed to permit a better arc of fire ahead. This group, together with the purchased *Stour* and *Test*, were the only British destroyers to have this arrangement, which proved to be generally unsatisfactory owing to the very wet position. Note the large W/T yard.

34. *Stour* and *Test* (the latter is shown, in 1912) were laid down by Lairds in 1903 as speculative construction and purchased by the Admiralty in December 1909 under the 1909/10 Programme to replace *Lee* and *Blackwater* lost that year. In all essentials they were identical to the *River*s but were completed with a modified armament of four 12pdrs and no 6pdrs.

35, 36. The twelve *Tribal* class boats, which were designed by individual builders to meet basic Admiralty requirements, were generally intended to meet Lord Fisher's demands for a large ocean-going destroyer type. On completion, the group were the largest and fastest destroyers in the world, but the price paid for their high speed was a weak armament in relation to the displacement and the type was not altogether successful – and was too expensive to be repeated. *Amazon* is seen here in all-black finish shortly before the war.

36▼

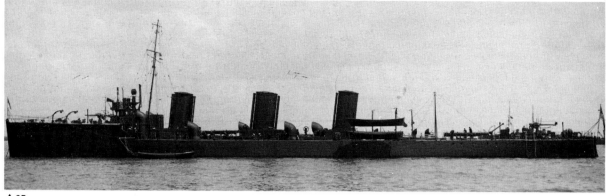

▲37

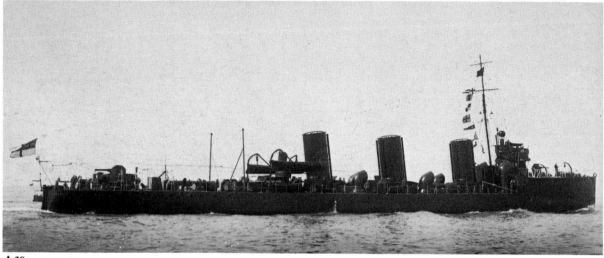

▲38

37, 38. The *Tribal*s proved to be fair seaboats, although the abnormally short forecastle in the majority of the class allowed the bow wave to ship inboard at high speed, making the decks very wet and uncomfortable. *Cossack* (shown) was completed in November 1907 and served with the Home Fleet until the outbreak of war in August 1914, after which she operated with the Dover Patrol until 1918. On 1 July 1917 she was in a collision and her depth charges

exploded, blowing off her stern. She was sold in December 1919.
39. The first five *Tribal*s were armed with three 12pdr guns, but two of the substantially better 4in weapons were fitted to each of the last seven boats, making them the first British destroyers to mount this armament. This improvement was still considered inadequate, however, and the general opinion was that the *Tribal*s could easily carry more than two of these guns. This is *Crusader*.

▼39

40▲

41▲

40. *Gurkha* running steam trials, when she attained a speed of 33.91kts. The entire class served in the Dover Patrol from 1914 until 1918, and taken as a whole it can be said that no other British destroyers saw more continual service, had more contact with the enemy or suffered more damage. *Gurkha* was lost when she struck a mine on 8 February 1917.
41. To test the structural strength of the *Tribal* class, *Mohawk* was subjected to severe weather conditions in the North Sea. The trials proved successful, and her hull showed no signs of weakness. *Mohawk* was mined off Dover on 1 June 1915 but managed to reach port, and she was later damaged by shellfire in action with enemy torpedo boat destroyers during the night of 26/27 October 1916 but survived this as well. She was sold after the war, in May 1919.
42. Built by Thornycroft and completed in 1909, *Nubian* served with the Home Fleet until the outbreak of war, but formed part of the Dover Patrol from August 1914 until October 1916.
On 26 October 1916 she had her bows blown off by a torpedo during an action with enemy torpedo boat destroyers. She was taken in tow, but the tow rope parted in bad weather and she ran aground near the South Foreland. See also photograph 46.

42▼

43. That the *Tribal* class were large, fine-looking vessels is clearly shown by this photograph of *Maori* in 1912. They were all engined by their respective builders, to an identical pattern so as to have all parts interchangeable, and were the first turbine-driven destroyers built for the Royal Navy as a class. *Maori* sank after hitting a mine off the Belgian coast on 7 May 1915.

▲ 44   ▼ 45

44. *Viking* – a lucky ship if ever there was one! Shortly after the outbreak of war she was damaged by gunfire from coastal batteries; on 29 December 1915 (as shown) she ran across a mine which blew off her stern (*Zulu* is standing by); whilst in dock under refit she blew up and had to be partly rebuilt; and in early 1918 she was rammed and badly damaged by a 'Q' ship. Surviving the war, she was finally sold to Wards in December 1919.

45. A prewar view of *Viking*. Note the straight stem, the high forecastle with strong upward sheer, and the turtle-back deck. The six short, thin, unevenly spaced funnels gave her a unique appearance – in fact, she was the only British warship ever to have six funnels. The 4in gun on the forecastle was later temporarily replaced by a 6in weapon.

46. After *Nubian* (photograph 42) had been salvaged, it was decided to cut her after section away and join it to the front part of *Zulu*, which had been heavily damaged in the stern by a mine in 1916. The two parts were united at Chatham Dockyard during 1916–17, and the vessel was commissioned as *Zubian* on 2 July 1917. Never quite as successful as other destroyers, she nevertheless did sterling service for the rest of the war, and on 4 February 1918 sank *UC50* by depth charge off Dungeness. She subsequently took part in the Zeebrugge and Ostend operations, and was finally sold in December 1919.

▲47

47. Built as an experiment to provide data for the construction of a new class of true ocean-going destroyers, *Swift* was the only one of her type. At 2,390 tons at deep load, she was rightfully classed as the first of the destroyer 'leaders'. She is seen here during her trials period in September 1909, when she attained 35.037kts at full power.

48. War modifications to *Swift* included a new foremast and topmast and the fitting of a searchlight on a platform behind the funnel. *Swift*'s proportions were not equalled until the *Tribals* of the 1936 Estimates were laid down. The submarine *K5* occupies the foreground.

49. *Swift* in 1917, after her two single 4in guns forward had been removed and replaced by a single 6in mounting. This arrangement

proved unsuccessful owing to problems with training and elevation.

50. The sixteen boats of the *Beagle* class formed the Estimates for the 1908/09 destroyer programme. The class initiated the policy of building destroyer groups to fixed standards of Admiralty design – eschewing the considerable latitude previously allowed to individual builders – although there were slight variations in detail. Being a compromise between the *Rivers* and the *Tribals*, they ended up being criticized as poor value for displacement with respect to their armament and speed; on the other hand they were very strongly built, reliable seaboats, and at last reasonably habitable. They were known in the Royal Navy as the 'Mediterranean Beagles'. The name-ship is shown here during the Dardanelles campaign in 1915.

▼48

49▲

50▲

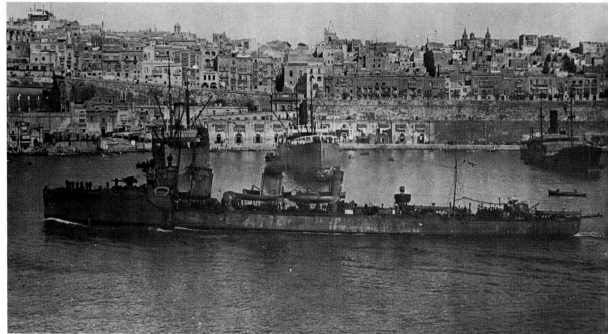

▲51

51. *Grampus* started life as *Nautilus* but was rechristened in the spring of 1914 to release the name for a new submarine. She is seen here entering Grand Harbour, Malta, in 1916. The original design for the group showed five 12pdrs, but a single 4in gun was substituted for the two forward 12pdr mountings while the boats were under construction. The *Beagle*s were the last coal-burning destroyers built for the Royal Navy.

52. In appearance the *Beagle* class vessels were all very much alike, although some differences in funnel design were evident. The first two funnels were noticeably thinner than the third, and it has been reported that the CO of *Scorpion* disliked the arrangement to the extent that he persuaded the dockyard to fit an extra steam pipe to disguise the fact. The group could be distinguished from all other British destroyers by having their torpedo tubes right aft as seen in this 1911 photograph of *Grasshopper*.

53. The *Beagle* class served with the Home Fleet (1st and 3rd DF) until early November 1913, and then transferred to the Mediterranean as the 5th DF, but *Beagle, Bulldog, Foxhound, Grasshopper, Pincher, Rattlesnake, Savage* and *Scourge* all returned home during September–November 1914 to serve with the

Portsmouth DF. They rejoined the 5th DF in the Mediterranean in April 1915 for the Dardanelles operations, the majority of the class taking part in that campaign and being very hard worked throughout. *Pincher*, seen here whilst in the Mediterranean in either 1913 or 1914, served with the British Aegean Squadron during 1916 and was then transferred back to Malta. She ended her career when she was wrecked on Seven Stones on 24 July 1918.

54. *Savage*, completed by Thornycroft in August 1910, took part in the bombardment of Akaba on 1 November 1914 and was then at the Dardanelles, where she bombarded the Turkish positions as well as performing convoy duties. She was also used as a minesweeper early in 1915, and was one of the vessels which took part in the occupation of Salamis during September and October 1916. She is shown in 1916, whilst in the Mediterranean.

55. A wartime view of *Scourge*. Note the raised forecastle, the slightly cutaway stern asnd the tall, slightly raking funnels, evenly spaced with the first two noticeably thicker than the third. Also of interest is the forecastle gun, which is prominently raised on a high breastwork.

▼52

53▲

54▲   55▼

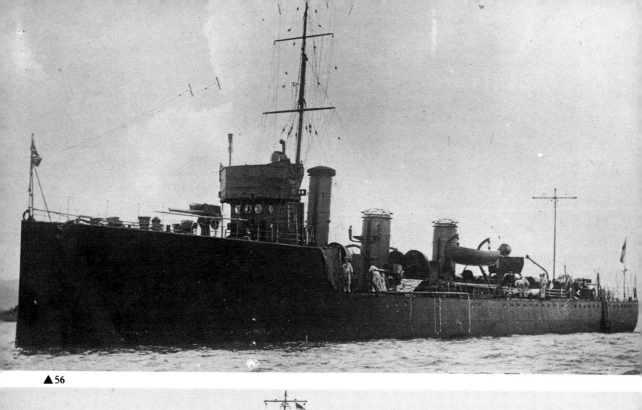

▲56

▲57 ▼58

56. The *Acorn* class were slightly smaller versions of the *Beagle*s, with a heavier gun armament, oil fuel instead of coal, and small detail modifications. The dimensions varied according to builders, but the general hull design was uniform throughout the class. This is *Acorn* in 1912; note the prominent caging to the funnel tops.

57. The gun armament in the *Acorn* class was improved over the *Beagle*s by substituting a 4in gun for the after 12pdr; the midships 2pdrs were rearranged abreast instead of *en echelon*, and the after torpedo tubes were located immediately abaft the forward tube instead of right at the stern. The twenty boats of the class received criticism similar to that directed at the *Beagle*s because they were given the same designed speed, which was thought by many to be inadequate for general destroyer work. Some units of the class, however, exceeded 29kts on preliminary trials, and several others reached 28kts. *Sheldrake* is seen here in June 1912.

58. The *Acheron* class initiated the practice of providing separate Admiralty and private builders' designs within each group: fourteen Admiralty boats were provided under the 1910/11 Programme, and six private boats under the same Estimates. The construction of the group came about through representations from Sir Alfred Yarrow and others to the effect that the average 27kts of contemporary British destroyers was quite inadequate when compared with the 30kts of the new German destroyers. *Archer* is shown running steam trials in 1912, when she made 28kts with 16,000shp.

59. *Beaver* of the *Acheron* class was built by Denny and was completed in 1912. She joined the Home Fleet (1st Fleet) until the outbreak of war, when she was transferred to the Harwich Force (1st DF). The photograph shows her in the North Sea: note the camouflaged forefunnel and the unusual rig.

60. *Oak*, *Lurcher* and *Firedrake* were special boats built to replace those Admiralty group destroyers which were transferred to the Royal Australian Navy on completion. The design represented a second Yarrow modification of the Admiralty type, with a 22ft increase in length, finer lines and substantially higher power and speed. The three vessels proved very successful throughout the war, and were regarded as 'crack ships' in the service. *Firedrake* is seen here in 1913 or 1914.

▲ 61

▲ 62

61. *Jackal*, another of the Admiralty *Acheron*s, seen in Malta just after the war. The paintwork consists of a very dark grey hull, with light grey upperworks.
62. *Phoenix*, seen here in 1917, saw action with German light cruisers off Heligoland on 16 August 1914, served with the Dover Patrol from October 1916 to March 1917 (during which time this photo was taken) and served with the British Aegean Squadron in January 1918. She was torpedoed and sunk by the Austrian

submarine *U28* in the Adriatic on 14 May 1918.
63. The *Acasta* class were a natural development from the *Acheron*s, and somewhat larger than the Admiralty group of that class. A third 4in gun was fitted, replacing the two 2pdrs. Thirteen boats were built to the Admiralty design, and seven in private yards. *Acasta* was present at the Battle of Dogger Bank in January 1915, and also at Jutland in May 1916, when she was heavily damaged and had to be towed home to be virtually rebuilt.

▼ 63

64▲

65▲

64. *Hardy* was one of the *Acasta* class 'specials' built by Thornycroft and completed in 1914. *Fortune, Hardy, Garland, Paragon, Porpoise, Unity* and *Victor*, all built by private yards, were generally 1–3kts faster than the Admiralty group and with the exception of *Fortune* differed only slightly. This boat, although officially included in the group, was actually a prototype for the three-funnelled 'L' class. *Hardy* (shown) was in action with enemy cruisers and torpedo boat destroyers during the raid on Scarborough on 16 December 1914 and sustained some damage.

65. *Paragon*, April 1914. On 18 March 1917, while serving with the Dover Patrol, she was torpedoed and sunk in action with enemy destroyers which were raiding Dover. There were only ten survivors.

66. *Victor*, seen here on patrol in the North Sea in 1915, was one of the destroyers which escorted the armoured cruiser *Hampshire* on her ill-fated voyage in June 1916 when Lord Kitchener was lost with that vessel. *Victor* survived the war, and was the last of the class to be sold, in late 1923.

66▼

▲ 67

68▲

67. The 1912/13 Programme provided the vessels which formed the 'L' (or *Laforey*) class, all the boats bearing names beginning with that letter. The basic design combined features of both the *Acasta*s and the *Acheron*s, and as usual there were both Admiralty boats and those built by private yards to Admiralty requirements. *Laurel, Liberty, Lark, Landrail, Laverock* and *Linnet* had two funnels, the rest of the class three. This photograph shows the stern of *Lennox* after she was torpedoed on the 28 June 1915; note the camouflage on the funnel.

68. *Lennox* cleared for action, 17 October 1914.
69. The 'M' class (1913/14 Programme) were divided into two groups, six boats being Admiralty designs and seven 'specials' from private yards. They were slightly improved versions of the *Laforey* group, with an emphasis on speed, and nearly all made over 32kts on preliminary speed trials. *Mansfield*, built by Hawthorn Leslie as one of the 'specials', is shown here on her preliminary trials making 33.7kts on 28,255shp.

69 ▼

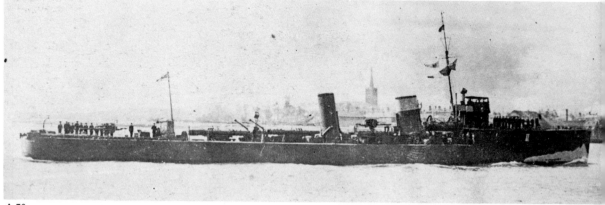

▲70

70. *Minos* was built by Yarrow and completed in 1914. This ship, along with *Miranda* and *Manly* (both of which were also built by Yarrow) was fitted with two funnels, but those built to the Admiralty design had three and the Hawthorn Leslie versions were fitted with four. *Minos* is seen here during the early months of 1915 and is sporting camouflage, which was not uncommon for destroyers throughout this period. Note the white-topped funnel to the fore and the false bow wave.

71. *Matchless*, one of the Admiralty 'Ms', seen in dry dock after striking a mine off Harwich on 9 November 1915 which blew off the whole of her stern. She had been towed home by her sister-ship *Murray*, and was under repair for over two months.

72. *Moorsom* was built by John Brown of Clydebank and is seen here on trials, when she attained a speed of 32.486kts. Note the 4in quick-firing (QF) gun, the compact bridgework with a 20in searchlight mounted on top, the three equal-sized funnels with the 4in gun between the third and fourth, and the 4in gun mounted right aft.

71▲   72▼

▲73

73. A photograph of *Milne* taken on 16 May 1917 while the ship was in dry dock at Dover, after she had rammed *UC26* near the Thames Estuary on 9 May. Note the small piece of submarine wedged in her bows.

74. *Mentor* running trials for her builder, Hawthorn Leslie. This boat and her sister *Mansfield* (see photo 69) were practically identical, although the former had a slightly lower bridge searchlight platform and could later be distinguished by the cap on her forefunnel.

75. A midships view of *Mentor*, showing her 4in mounting. Note the unusual way in which the funnel tops have been painted.

▼74

75▶

▲76

▲77

76. *Mentor* coming into port with badly damaged bows after she had struck a mine near the Horns Reef on 18 August 1915.
77. *Mentor* in trouble again, following a collision. Depite these mishaps she survived the war and was finally put up for sale in 1921.
78, 79. Powerfully armed with six 4in guns, *Tipperary* was one of the large destroyers built for the Chilean Navy and then taken over by the Royal Navy on completion; with her sisters *Faulknor*, *Broke* and *Botha*, she served as flotilla leader. *Tipperary* is shown here after being towed back to Harwich by *Lurcher* in 1915 with mine damage. Following repairs she was present at the Battle of Jutland, when she was wrecked and sunk by gunfire during the night action.
80. A need for flotilla leaders resulted in the seven vessels of the *Lightfoot* class, which were provided under the 1913/15 Programmes. There was an improvement in accommodation, and

signalling equipment was fitted as standard, whilst armament comprised four 4in guns instead of three. While *Abdiel* was fitting out it was decided to convert her to a minelayer, but to disguise this large canvas screens were placed around the mine rails, with torpedo tubes and 4in guns painted on the sides, as seen in the photograph.
81. *Kempenfelt* was built by Cammell Laird as a unit of the *Lightfoot* class. These ships were extremely strongly built, with exceptional subdivision for destroyers; all proved excellent seaboats, and were highly regarded in service. *Kempenfelt* was forced hard on her speed trials in 1915 and managed to reach nearly 35kts on over 37,000shp. The photograph was taken in late 1917; note the large bridgework and the tall, thin forefunnel.

▼78

79 ▲

80 ▲   81 ▼

▲82

▲83 ▼84

82. The Fleet at sea in 1917, with several destroyers in evidence. G10 is *Kempenfelt*, G16 *Mystic*, G05 *Marne* and G43 *Prince* The battleship in the background is *Royal Oak*.

83. *Talisman*, shown here on her speed trials early in 1916, was one of four ships allegedly built for the Turkish Navy by Hawthorn Leslie and then taken over by the Royal Navy. Powerfully armed ships, with five 4in guns and four 21in torpedo tubes, they resembled the British 'M' group in basic design. Note the two 4in guns on the forecastle deck.

84. *Minion* was one of twenty vessels ordered in September 1914, comprising sixteen Admiralty boats and four 'specials' from Yarrow. Armed with three 4in guns and four 21in torpedo tubes, they were virtual repeats of the original 'M' group but had their midships gun mounted on a raised platform to help keep the position dry in a seaway. The photograph shows *Minion* in 1916 or 1917 in her war rig.

85. *Minion* just after the cessation of hostilities, in 1919. Note the two sets of torpedo tubes amidships behind the funnels, the 4in guns aft and the minesweeping gear.

86. A wartime photograph dated about 1917 and showing (left to right) *Mons* (G11), *Napier*, *Mandate* (G02) and the flotilla leader *Seymour*.

85▲   86▼

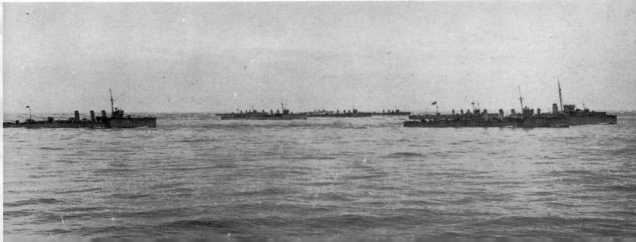

▲87

87. *Marmion* was built by Swan Hunter and completed at the end of
1915. The photograph, which shows her wearing camouflage
around her three funnels, was taken a few months before her loss on
21 October 1917, when she collided with *Tirade* and, despite an
attempt to tow her to port, foundered.

88. *Manners, Mandate, Magic, Moresby, Marmion, Martial, Mary
Rose* and *Menace* of the September 1914 group were fitted with
cruising turbines, in a move stipulated by the Admiralty when the
ships were first ordered to save time in the construction stage. The
rest of the class had either Parsons or Brown Curtis direct-drive
turbines.

89. *Magic*, about 1917. Note the 2pdr gun mounted in the tower
between the torpedo tubes instead of the usual 20in searchlight, and
also the pronounced 'step' between forecastle and main deck level.

90. *Moresby* leads one of the Thornycroft 'specials', followed by one
of the Yarrow 'specials'; all are members of the 'M' group. Note
how the straight stem helps to keep the forecastle dry. As completed
all these boats were practically identical, but individuals could be
distinguished by slight differences in bridgework, masts and yards,
as well as by the positions of their steam pipes.

91. *Musketeer*, built by Yarrow as one of the 'M' 'specials', is seen at
sea in company with the battleship *Orion* during a sweep early in
1918. Note how the bows take the water on board. *Moon, Morning
Star* and *Mounsley* were sister-ships to *Musketeer*; all were very
successful, and showed an increase in speed over the Admiralty
'M' class vessels.

▼88

89▲

90▲ 91▼

▲92

▲93 ▼94

92. *Moon* takes up her position with the Grand Fleet in Scapa Flow. Note the main steam sirens on the front of the forefunnel: these were identical in all Yarrow 'Ms' but in others of the group the location varied a great deal.

93. Another nine vessels conforming to the original Admiralty 'M' design were ordered in November 1914, with an allowance for just one 'special' from Yarrow. *Negro*, built by Palmers, is seen here leading the Battle Cruiser Squadron (BCS) to sea in about 1916; this particular ship was lost after a collision in the North Sea with *Hoste* during heavy weather on 21 December 1916.

94. *Nereus* speeding at over 30kts in choppy water, about 1917. Note the spray over the forecastle, which makes for a wet command in the 'A' gun position. The water that came aboard, however, quickly drained away, and these conditions did not hamper the efficiency of the position to any great extent.

95. A third order for 22 more 'Ms' came at the end of November 1914, but no provision for any 'special' within the group was made on this occasion. *Noble* is shown at anchor in 1917 under the Forth Bridge.

96. *Norman* in the winter of 1917, leaving Rosyth; *Peyton* is in the background.

97. *Opal* was built by Doxford and completed at the beginning of 1916. She is shown running trials on the Tyne, where she attained a speed of 34.31kts. The ship was completely wrecked during a gale in January 1918.

95▲

96▲ 97▼

▲ 98

98. *Oracle* displays her damage following a ramming encounter with the submarine *UC44* in the North Sea on 5 August 1917.

99. *Orford* wearing barely discernible Grand Fleet funnel bands and a hull number which is not one of the Grand Fleet markings. The photograph was taken late in 1918 or early 1919, when the destroyer was changing flotillas.

100. Eighteen further 'Ms' were provided for in the early part of 1915: *Parthian*, built by Scotts, is seen here on trials in 1916, when she made over 35kts. Note the almost vertical stem, a feature exclusive to *Nictator*, *Narwhal* and this ship; the others of the group had a more raked bow.

101. A view of *Pasley*, showing her starboard broadside (and giving a good impression of her layout).

▼ 99

100▲   101▼

102. An onboard photograph of *Pasley*, taken from behind the third funnel, when she had just begun to make smokescreen. Note the 21in torpedo tubes.
103. *Peyton*'s main deck looking aft while the vessel is at high speed. Note the 4in gun sponson behind the funnel.

◀102   103▶

▲ 104

104. *Peyton* was one of the 22 'M' class destroyers ordered in May 1915. Built by Denny, the ship is shown here in incredibly heavy weather and almost completely awash, which makes one wonder what conditions were like on board at this time.

105. *Pellew* (built by Beardmore) on her preliminary trials whilst making a sixteen-point turn at her full speed of 32kts.

106. Ninety vessels were built to the same basic requirements within the Admiralty 'M' group, all ordered under the emergency war programmes. They formed the 11th, 12th, 13th and 14th Flotillas and constituted the backbone of destroyer strength for the Royal Navy throughout the war. This is *Portia*, in 1917 or 1918.

▼ 105

107. A call for more flotilla leaders resulted in six vessels which in all essentials were repeats of the *Lightfoot* class. Improvements were made by moving the position of the bridge further aft and allowing superimposed 'A' and 'B' gun positions, which ensured a dry command for 'B' gun in almost all weather conditions. The two forward funnels were merged into one, which gave extra space for torpedo tubes and equipment aft as well as making for a unique appearance. *Seymour* is shown as completed in 1916; in November 1916 it was decided to convert this ship to a minelayer, as which she proved successful.

106▲   107▼

▲ 108

▼ 109

108. The basic requirements for the emergency war programme of during 1915 called for an improved 'M' class vessel, and with slight modifications such as an enlarged superstructure forward and a raised gun position aft, two dozen boats were ordered to this design. Seven 'specials' were provided, four by Yarrow and three from Thornycroft, whilst two 'M' class ships previously ordered from Swan Hunter were altered to become units of the same group. All were called the 'R' class, one of which, *Red Gauntlet*, is shown in this 1917 photograph.

109. *Parker* was one of the repeat *Lightfoot* leaders, and was originally to have been called *Frobisher*; she is shown as completed in 1916, at anchor in Scapa Flow. Note the superimposed 4in guns, with 'B' gun mounted on a short deck extended forward to protect crewmen serving 'A' gun. Noteworthy also are the crow's nest on the foremast, the tall, round shaped forward funnel, the smaller twin funnels aft and the torpedo tubes amidships. *Parker* survived the war, and was sold in 1921.

110. With a designed shaft horse power of 27,000 for an average speed of 36kts, the 'Rs' would be a match for most of the foreign contemporary torpedo boat destroyers, although as completed many of the group reached speeds far in excess of this: *Rocket* (shown here in 1917) made 35.66kts with 28,450shp.

110▲

▲111

111. *Sable* (shown) was broken up postwar and her name was transferred to a sister-ship, *Salmon*, in 1933. Another sister-ship, *Skate*, went on to serve in the Second World War as the oldest surviving 'R' class destroyer.

112. The Admiralty design within the 'R' group had three funnels, whilst those boats built by Yarrow had but two. *Sybille*, one of the 'specials', was the fastest 'R' class destroyer within the first group, making 39.11kts on her preliminary trials. Some sources refer to *Sybille* as a 'later M type' destroyer.

113. Fifty-one destroyers were built to the basic 'R' design and, on the whole, they proved to be excellent seaboats, adequate fighting vessels and generally efficient ships. *Tancred*, seen here in 1918, was one of the modified 'R' group which had improved boiler and machinery arrangements, three funnels and an improved 4in gun.

112▲ 113▼

59

▲ 114

114. *Tarpon*, built by John Brown as an 'R' and completed in 1917, is shown limping into port on 14 July 1917 after striking a mine off Dunkirk. The damage was so extensive that she was in dockyard hands for almost six months.

115. Built under the 1916/17 Programme, the 28 Admiralty 'V' class destroyers were basically improved 'Rs' and were probably the finest and most efficient destroyers in existence at the time of their entry into service. The first five within the group were built as leaders, based on *Seymour*. *Valkyrie* is shown here, in 1918.

116. The 'Vs' were approximately 235 tons heavier than the 'Rs', with a gun armament one-third heavier, the same number of torpedo tubes and about two knots' less speed. They were also 36ft longer overall and had nearly 3ft more beam. Note in this 1918 view of *Vega* the superimposed 4in Mk V guns forward, introduced in the *Seymour* group. This fitting was also given to the aft mounting in the 'Vs' by moving the third gun from amidships to aft and raising it – an adaptation that made these boats unique. The bow damage visible was incurred when *Vega* rammed a submarine.

▼ 115

▲117
117. *Vendetta* in the Firth of Forth, 1918. Built by Fairfield and completed in October 1917, she was with the Grand Fleet until March 1919, taking part in the Second Battle of Heligoland Bight on 17 November 1917 and in the capture of Bolshevik destroyers in the Baltic on 26/27 December 1918. She served in the Mediterranean from 1924 until 1932 and in 1937 was transferred to the Royal Australian Navy, remaining on strength until 1948.
118. *Vanoc*, seen here on trials in the summer of 1917, was converted for minelaying duties in June 1918 and laid 965 mines

from June to November 1918. She served with the Royal Navy for almost thirty years before being sold for scrapping in July 1945, although she cheated the scrapyard after becoming wrecked off Cornwall in June 1946 whilst under tow.
119. *Vittoria* was another 'V' converted for minelaying duties. Whilst serving with the 20th DF she was torpedoed and sunk by a Russian submarine off Seskan Island on 31 August 1919. She sank in just over five minutes, but all but eight of her crew were rescued.

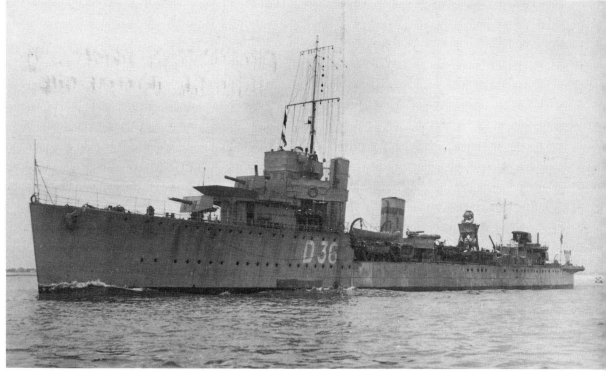

▲ 120

120. The 'V' class were designed for 34kts (on 27,000shp), which gave them a nominal speed the same as that of the *Seymour* group and 'M' class but 2kts less than that of the 'Rs'. However, the special Admiralty requirement regarding speed was that they should be able to maintain 25kts in any weather in which capital ships could steam at full speed (i.e., 21–22kts). *Vivacious*, shown, made

▼ 121

33.01kts on trials in deep load condition.

121. Except for triple instead of twin torpedo tubes and a tall mainmast to accommodate improved W/T, the 'Ws' were repeats of the 'Vs'. *Walpole*, built by Doxford and completed in August 1918, scouted with the Grand Fleet until March 1919. She served in the Second World War and was sold for scrapping in March 1945.